FAVOURITE ENGLISH PUDDING RECIPES

Traditional
Baked, Boiled and
Steamed Desserts

*With illustrations of
household life*

SALMON

Index

Apple & Bramble Crumble   18
Baked Jam Roll   37
Blackcap Pudding   40
Brown Betty   29
Castle Puddings   13
Cherry Pudding   47
Chester Pudding   19
Chiltern Hills Pudding   26
Clootie Dumpling   8
Coffee & Walnut Pudding   5
Cumberland Apple Pudding   27
Duffield Batter Pudding   34
Elderberry Pie   11
Fig Dumpling   35
Folkestone Pudding Pie   38
Ginger Marmalade Pudding   45
Huntingdon Pudding   42

Marmalade Batter Pudding   6
Marquis Pudding   46
Monmouth Pudding   43
Newcastle Pudding   14
Plum Duff   22
Queen of Puddings   3
Raspberry Sponge Pudding   7
Rochester Pudding   16
"Stir-in" Pudding   39
Summer Pudding   32
Vectis Pudding   30
Vegetable Plum Pudding   24
Warwick Pudding   10
Welsh Rice Pudding   21
West Country Tart   15
Wet Nelly   31
White Ladies Pudding   23

Cover pictures *front:* "Breakfast" by *Edward Thompson Davis*
back: "A Calm Sea" by *William Henry Midwood*
Title page: "A Quiet Moment" by *Henry Benjamin Roberts R.I.*

Printed and Published by J. Salmon Ltd., Sevenoaks, England © Copyright

Queen of Puddings

A baked sponge coated with raspberry jam and with a meringue topping.

4 oz fresh white breadcrumbs	**½ pint milk**
½ oz butter, softened	**2 eggs, separated**
4 oz caster sugar	**1-2 tablespoons raspberry jam**
Grated rind of ½ a lemon	**Caster sugar for sprinkling**

Set oven to 350°F or Mark 4. Butter a 1 pint pie dish. Put the breadcrumbs, butter, 1 oz of the sugar and the lemon rind into a bowl and mix together. Heat the milk in a pan and pour over the breadcrumb mixture. Beat the egg yolks and mix into the breadcrumbs. Pour into the pie dish and bake for about 35 minutes until set. Remove from the oven and spread the jam in a layer on top of the pudding. Reduce oven to 300°F or Mark 2. Whisk the egg whites stiffly and fold in the remaining 3 oz sugar. Pile this meringue mixture on top of the jam layer and sprinkle with caster sugar. Bake for about another 30 minutes until the meringue is firm and brown on top. Serves 4.

Coffee and Walnut Pudding

A steamed sponge pudding with a distinctive flavour and a nutty texture.

4 oz butter, softened	4 oz flour
4 oz sugar	Pinch of salt
2 eggs, beaten	1 tablespoon coffee essence

2 oz chopped walnuts

Grease a 2 pint pudding basin. Cream the butter and sugar together in a bowl until light and fluffy. Beat in the eggs a little at a time and then fold in the flour and salt. Add the coffee essence and chopped walnuts and combine well together. Put into the basin, cover with buttered greaseproof paper and cover and seal with kitchen foil. Steam for 1½ to 2 hours, topping up the water as necessary. Turn out on to a warm plate and serve with butterscotch sauce. Serves 4 to 6.

Alternatively, substitute 2 oz cocoa powder and 2 tablespoons of milk for the coffee and walnuts to make a chocolate pudding.

Marmalade Batter Pudding

A light soufflé type of pudding coated with marmalade and flavoured with ginger.

6 oz flour	Grated rind of ½ a lemon
Pinch of salt	Grated rind of ½ an orange
2 oz caster sugar	4 eggs, separated
½ teaspoon ground ginger	1 pint milk

2-3 oz orange marmalade

Set oven to 400°F or Mark 6. Sift the flour and salt into a bowl and mix in the sugar, ginger and lemon and orange rind. Mix in the egg yolks and milk and beat to a smooth batter. Whisk the egg whites stiffly to hold their peaks and carefully fold into the mixture. Line an ovenproof dish with the marmalade and pour in the batter. Bake for about 20 minutes until risen and set. Serve with warmed marmalade sauce. Serves 4 to 6.

Raspberry Sponge Pudding

Raspberries embedded in a baked light sponge – a perfect summer fruit pudding.

8 oz raspberries   **1 egg, separated**
4 oz butter   **½ pint milk**
3 oz caster sugar   **8 oz self raising flour**
Pinch of salt

Set oven to 400°F or Mark 6. Well butter a 7½ inch square baking tin. Carefully pick over the raspberries and discard any that are damaged. Cream together the butter and sugar in a bowl until light and fluffy. Beat the egg yolk, add to the creamed mixture and beat well. Stir in the milk. Sieve together the flour and salt and fold into the mixture a little at a time. Fold in the raspberries. Whisk the egg white until stiff and carefully fold into the mixture. Pour into the tin, spread out and bake for about 30 minutes until golden. Turn out on to a warm dish and serve sliced with cream. Serves 4.

Clootie Dumpling

This Scottish steamed fruit pudding would traditionally have been cooked in a cloth or "clout" – hence the name Clootie Dumpling.

4 oz self raising flour	1 oz chopped mixed peel
2 oz fresh white breadcrumbs	2 oz soft brown sugar
3 oz shredded suet	1 teaspoon mixed spice
2 oz sultanas	1 egg, lightly beaten
2 oz currants	1 tablespoon golden syrup

4 fl.oz milk

Grease a large pudding basin. In a bowl, mix together all the dry ingredients. Stir in the beaten egg and golden syrup with sufficient milk to produce a soft consistency. Put the mixture into the basin, allowing plenty of room for it to swell. Cover with buttered greaseproof paper and cover and seal with kitchen foil. Steam for about 2 hours, topping up the water as necessary. Turn out on to a warmed plate and serve with whipped cream and warmed golden syrup. Serves 4.

'Fireside Contentment' by Henry J. Dobson R.S.W.

Warwick Pudding

A custard pudding containing dried figs, ginger and ginger wine.

4 tablespoons ginger wine
2 oz dried figs, trimmed and very finely chopped
½ pint milk   3 egg yolks   2 oz caster sugar
1 oz gelatine   4 tablespoons water   ½ pint double cream
1 oz preserved ginger, very finely chopped
Whipped cream for decoration

Overnight, soak the chopped figs in the ginger wine. Next day, drain off the wine from the figs and set both aside. Put the milk into a saucepan and heat until almost boiling. Whisk the egg yolks and sugar together and stir into the milk, combining well. Stir gently over a low heat until the custard is creamy, then allow to cool. Put the gelatine in a cup with the water and stand in a saucepan of hot water, stirring gently until the gelatine has dissolved and is syrupy. Stir the melted gelatine into the ginger wine and set aside until lukewarm. Whip the cream until it stands in soft peaks. Stir the gelatine into the custard, then combine together the custard and the cream, whisking well. Leave to cool and thicken, then stir in the chopped ginger. Add the drained figs, stir lightly, pour into a glass serving bowl and leave to set. Decorate with rosettes of whipped cream. Serve with pouring cream. Serves 4 to 6.

Elderberry Pie

Elderberries are a prolific summer wild fruit which can easily be made into this simple plate pie.

8 oz sweet shortcrust pastry
1 lb elderberries, strigged, washed and dried
3 oz sugar (or more according to taste)   1 tablespoon cornflour
Juice of ½ a lemon   1 small beaten egg for glazing
Caster sugar for sprinkling

Set oven to 375ºF or Mark 5. Butter an 8 inch pie plate. Roll out the pastry on a lightly floured surface and use half to line the pie plate. Prepare the elderberries and mix with the sugar, cornflour and lemon juice. Put the fruit mixture on to the pastry and spread out evenly. Moisten the edge, cover with a lid of the remaining pastry and trim and seal the edge. Cut a steam hole and brush with beaten egg. Bake for about 30 minutes until the pastry is golden. Sprinkle the top with caster sugar and serve with double cream. Serves 4 to 6.

Castle Puddings

These individual steamed sponge puddings originated at the Royal House of Hanover;
"Castle" is an English corruption of the German "Kassel".

4 oz butter, softened	**4 oz flour**
4 oz sugar	**Pinch of salt**
2 eggs, beaten	**Grated rind of 1 lemon**

Grease 8 dariole moulds. Cream together the butter and sugar in a bowl until light and fluffy. Beat in the eggs, a little at a time with a little flour. Fold in the remaining flour, salt and lemon rind and mix thoroughly. Divide the mixture between the moulds, cover with buttered greaseproof paper and cover and seal with kitchen foil and steam for 30 to 40 minutes topping up the water as necessary. Turn out and serve with lemon sauce (see page 14). Serves 6 to 8.

Alternatively, omit the lemon rind and serve with warmed jam or golden syrup.

Newcastle Pudding

A steamed form of bread-and-butter pudding, flavoured with lemon and served with a slightly tart lemon sauce.

**¾ pint milk   Grated rind of 1 lemon   3 eggs, beaten   2 oz sugar
6 slices white bread with crusts removed and thickly buttered**

Well butter a 1 to 1½ pint pudding basin. Warm the milk in a pan, stir in the lemon rind, cover and leave to infuse for about an hour. When ready, beat the eggs and sugar together in a bowl, pour in the milk and whisk briskly. Line the pudding basin with the slices of bread, buttered side inwards. Strain the milk mixture into the basin and leave to soak for about an hour. Cover with buttered greaseproof paper and cover and seal with kitchen foil. Steam for 40 to 45 minutes, topping up the water as necessary. Serve with Lemon Sauce. Serves 4.

Lemon Sauce:
**2 oz caster sugar   1 pint water   Rind and juice of 1 lemon
2 beaten eggs   3 oz butter**

Boil together the sugar, water and lemon rind until slightly reduced and thickened. Stand the pan in a pan of boiling water, stir in the eggs and butter and whisk continually until the sauce thickens. Strain and serve hot.

West Country Tart

A treacle tart filled with chopped walnuts.

6 oz shortcrust pastry

FILLING
8 oz golden syrup   1 oz soft brown sugar
3 oz walnuts, finely chopped   2 medium eggs

TOPPING
2 oz flour   1 oz butter, softened   1 tablespoon caster sugar

Set oven to 350°F or Mark 4. Grease a 7 inch flan dish. Roll out the pastry on a floured surface and use to line the dish, trimming the edge. Warm the golden syrup. Mix together in a bowl the golden syrup, brown sugar and the eggs and spoon the mixture over the pastry base. Make the topping in another bowl by rubbing the butter into the flour and then stir in the caster sugar. Sprinkle the topping evenly over the syrup mixture and bake for about 30 minutes until golden. Serve with double cream. Serves 4.

Rochester Pudding

An old-fashioned treacle sponge pudding; golden syrup can be substituted if preferred.

6 oz self raising flour	Pinch of salt
3 oz butter, softened	1 egg, beaten
3 oz sugar	2 to 3 tablespoons milk
6 oz black treacle or golden syrup	

Well grease a 2 pint pudding basin. Sift the flour into a bowl and rub in the butter until the mixture resembles breadcrumbs. Add the sugar and salt and mix to a soft, dropping consistency with the beaten egg and sufficient of the milk. Line the basin with the treacle or golden syrup and pour in the sponge mixture. Cover with buttered greaseproof paper and cover and seal with kitchen foil. Steam for $1\frac{1}{2}$ to 2 hours and turn out on to a warm plate. Serve with warmed treacle or syrup or with custard. Serves 4 to 6.

'Morning Lessons' *by William Bromley*

Apple and Bramble Crumble

Apples and blackberries always combine well together.

1 lb cooking apples, peeled, cored and sliced
8 oz blackberries
4-6 oz granulated sugar, to taste

CRUMBLE
4 oz flour   2 oz porridge oats   Pinch of salt
4 oz butter   4 oz Demerara sugar

Set oven to 375°F or Mark 5. Mix together the apples and blackberries and put into a pie dish. Add the sugar according to taste and a very little water. For the crumble, put the flour, oats, salt and butter into a bowl and work together with the hands until the mixture resembles breadcrumbs. Stir in the Demerara sugar and sprinkle the crumble mixture over the fruit. Bake for about 15 minutes and then reduce the temperature to 350°F or Mark 4 and bake for a further 35 to 40 minutes or until the top is lightly browned. Serve with double cream. Serves 4.

Chester Pudding

A steamed suet pudding incorporating rum-flavoured blackcurrant jam.

4 oz self raising flour	1 teaspoon rum (optional)
4 oz shredded suet	2 oz caster sugar
4 oz fresh white breadcrumbs	1 egg, beaten
4 oz blackcurrant jam	Milk to mix

Well butter a 2 pint pudding basin. In a bowl, mix together the flour, suet and breadcrumbs. Stir together the jam and rum, if desired, and add to the mixture, combining well. Stir in the sugar and the beaten egg. Mix to a soft dough with a little milk, then spoon into the basin. Cover with greaseproof paper and cover and seal with kitchen foil. Steam for 3 hours, topping up the water as necessary. Turn out on to a warm dish and serve accompanied by a sauce made of warmed blackcurrant jam, flavoured, if desired, with a little rum. Serves 4 to 6.

Welsh Rice Pudding

This rice pudding is lightened with stiffly beaten egg white and flavoured with nutmeg and a bayleaf.

1 pint milk	**A small bayleaf**
¼ teaspoon ground nutmeg	**1½ oz pudding rice**
Pinch of salt	**2 eggs, separated**

Lightly butter a 1½ to 2 pint pie dish. Pour the milk into a saucepan, add the nutmeg, salt and bayleaf and bring to the boil. Stir in the rice and simmer until the milk is absorbed and the rice cooked, adding a little extra milk if necessary. Remove from the heat and discard the bayleaf. Set oven to 425°F or Mark 7. Allow the rice to cool slightly then mix in the egg yolks. Whisk the egg whites until they hold their shape and fold into the rice mixture. Put into the dish and bake for 10 to 15 minutes or until the top is golden. Serve with stewed fruit, jam or honey. Serves 4.

This rice pudding contains no sugar. However, if desired, a little sugar can be added according to taste.

Plum Duff

*This boiled suet pudding dates from the early years of the 19th century. "Duff" is
a colloquial corruption of dough and dried plums were originally used, as
in Plum Pudding. It is very simple to make.*

8 oz flour	**3 oz caster sugar**
2 teaspoons baking powder	**4 oz shredded suet**
1 teaspoon mixed spice	**6 oz raisins**
6 fl.oz milk	

Sift the flour and baking powder into a bowl and mix in the spice, sugar, suet and
raisins. Stir in the milk and blend thoroughly. Roll the pudding mixture in buttered
greaseproof paper and then in a clean, floured pudding cloth and tie the ends, but
leave plenty of room for the pudding to swell. Lower into a pan of boiling water,
cover and boil for 2½ to 3 hours, topping up the water as necessary. Serve cut into
slices, with custard. Serves 4 to 6.

White Ladies Pudding

A variation of bread and butter pudding made with the addition of desiccated coconut.

3 oz desiccated coconut
5-6 slices of white bread, thickly buttered
½ pint milk   Vanilla essence   Pinch of salt
2 eggs   2 oz sugar

Set oven to 350°F or Mark 4. Butter a 1½ to 2 pint pie dish and sprinkle thickly with the desiccated coconut. Remove the crusts from the bread and cut into squares or triangles and arrange in the dish. Heat the milk in a saucepan and add a few drops of vanilla essence and a pinch of salt. Beat the eggs in a bowl with the sugar, then pour in the milk and stir well. Strain the milk mixture over the bread in the pie dish and leave to soak for 30 minutes. Then place the pie dish in a *bain-mairie* of boiling water and bake for 30 to 40 minutes until set and browned on top. Serves 4 to 6.

Vegetable Plum Pudding

A steamed suet pudding made with grated carrot and potato, with the addition of dried fruit. White flour and sugar can be substituted if preferred.

2 oz wholemeal flour	**2 oz shredded suet**
Pinch of salt	**1 oz raisins**
2 oz grated carrot	**1 oz currants**
2 oz grated potato	**1 egg, beaten**
2 oz soft brown sugar	**1-2 tablespoons milk**

Grease a 1 to 1½ pint pudding basin. Grate the vegetables. Put all the ingredients together into a large bowl and mix thoroughly. Spoon into the basin, cover with buttered greaseproof paper and cover and seal with kitchen foil. Steam for about 3 hours, topping up the water as necessary. Turn out onto a warm plate and serve with a sweet white sauce or with custard. Serves 4.

'Peeling Potatoes' by Carlton Alfred Smith R.I.

Chiltern Hills Pudding

A steamed pudding containing dried fruit, suet and tapioca.

**2 oz tapioca   ¼ pint milk   1 tablespoon single cream
4 oz shredded suet   4 oz raisins or sultanas
1 teaspoon bicarbonate of soda dissolved in a little milk
4 oz fresh white breadcrumbs   3 oz sugar
A few drops of vanilla essence**

Well butter a 2 to 2½ pint pudding basin. In a bowl, soak the tapioca in the milk for 2 hours, then stir in the cream. Mix together the suet and the dried fruit. Add the dissolved bicarbonate of soda to the tapioca, then stir in the suet mixture, breadcrumbs, sugar and vanilla essence. Spoon into the basin, cover with buttered greaseproof paper and cover and seal with kitchen foil. Steam for 2½ to 3 hours, topping up the water as necessary. Turn out onto a warm plate and serve with cream, custard or vanilla sauce. Serves 4 to 6.

Cumberland Apple Pudding

A ginger flavoured apple crumble.

**1½ lb cooking apples, peeled, cored and sliced   Sugar to taste
8 oz self raising flour   Pinch of salt   1 teaspoon ground ginger
4 oz butter, softened   4 oz soft brown sugar**

Set over to 375°F or Mark 5. Butter a large pie dish. Stew the apples with just a very little water and with sufficient sugar to taste, until soft. Put the stewed apples in the pie dish. Sieve the flour, salt and ginger into a bowl, rub in the butter and stir in the sugar. Spread the mixture over the apples and bake for about 30 minutes until browned on top. Serve with cream or custard. Serves 4 to 6.

Brown Betty

An old-fashioned layered pudding of apples, breadcrumbs and golden syrup.

1 lb cooking apples   4 oz fresh brown breadcrumbs
2 oz Demerara sugar   ½ teaspoon mixed spice
3 tablespoons golden syrup   Grated rind and juice of ½ a lemon

Set oven to 350°F or Mark 4. Grease a 2 to 2½ pint pie dish. Peel and core the apples and slice thinly. Mix together the sugar and mixed spice. Put a layer of apple slices in the dish, cover with a layer of breadcrumbs, sprinkle with sugar and cover with a spoonful of golden syrup. Repeat the layers until the ingredients are used up. Add the lemon juice and sprinkle over the grated lemon rind. Bake for about 30 minutes until browned and bubbling. Serve with cream. Serves 4.

'The Keeper's Daughter' *by William Shayer*

Vectis Pudding

A steamed suet roll with currants, apple and black treacle.
Vectis is the Roman name for the Isle of Wight.

8 oz prepared sweet suet pastry   4 oz black treacle
1½-2 oz currants   1 cooking apple, peeled, cored and chopped
Grated rind of half a lemon   ½-1 teaspoon mixed spice

Roll out the pastry about ¼ inch thick on a lightly floured surface to form a strip 8 to 10 inches long. Spread the treacle to within ½ to 1 inch of the edges then arrange the currants and apple evenly over the top. Sprinkle with the lemon rind mixed with the spice. Moisten the edges of the pastry, roll up carefully from a long side and seal the edges well. Roll up in buttered greaseproof paper and then in a clean, floured pudding cloth and tie the ends, but leave plenty of room for the pudding to swell. Steam for 2 hours, topping up the water as necessary. Serve cut into slices, with cream or custard. Serves 4 to 6.

Wet Nelly

This Northern version of Bread Pudding was originally made with crusts left over from making bread sauce. Party sandwiches are another source of crusts.

8 oz fresh white breadcrumbs	**4 oz shredded suet**
5 fl.oz milk	**4 oz soft brown sugar**
2 teaspoons mixed spice	**Butter for dotting**
Grated rind of ½ a lemon	**Extra brown sugar for sprinkling**

Soak the breadcrumbs in the milk for about 30 minutes. Set oven to 350ºF or Mark 4. Well grease a 7 to 8 inch baking tin. Stir into the soaked breadcrumbs the mixed spice, lemon rind, suet and brown sugar and combine well together. Put the mixture into the tin, spread out evenly and smooth the surface. Dot with butter and sprinkle with brown sugar. Bake for 1 to 1½ hours until firm and golden. Cut into slices and serve hot or cold with custard. Serves 4.

Summer Pudding

This delicious and quintessentially English cold pudding consists of a bread lining soaked with lightly cooked and juicy summer soft fruits.

1-1½ lb fruit (a mixture of raspberries, strawberries, redcurrants and blackcurrants)
Sugar to taste   Scant ¼ pint water   4-6 slices medium sliced bread
5 oz whipped cream

Take a 2 pint pudding basin or soufflé dish. Put the currants with sufficient sugar to taste into a pan with the water. Simmer gently until almost soft, add the raspberries and strawberries and cook for a further 3 minutes. Meanwhile, cut the crusts off the bread and then cut the bread to fit the base and sides of the dish. Put the fruit mixture into the basin, reserving 2 to 3 fl.oz of the juice. Top with the remaining bread, pressing down firmly. Cover the basin with a plate or saucer to fit the top exactly, place about a 1lb weight on top and leave in the refrigerator overnight. Turn out on to a serving dish just before serving and use the reserved juice to cover any parts of the bread which have remained white. Serve with whipped cream. Serves 4 to 6.

'The Little Gardener' by George Bernard O'Neill

Duffield Batter Pudding

This baked stewed fruit and batter pudding comes from Derbyshire.
Alternatively it can be steamed in a pudding basin.

4 oz flour   1 oz melted butter
1 pint milk   3 eggs, beaten
Fresh stewed fruit as available or a tin of fruit

Set oven to 350°F or Mark 4. Grease an ovenproof dish and spread the drained fruit over the base. Sieve the flour into a bowl, moisten with a little milk, stir in the melted butter and the beaten eggs and then gradually beat in the remaining milk. Pour the batter mixture over the fruit and bake for about 50 minutes until set and golden brown. Serve warm with cream or ice cream. Serves 4.

Fig Dumpling

Dried figs make a change of flavour from the more usual dried fruit that is used in steamed puddings.

6 oz dried figs, trimmed and chopped　**6 oz sugar**
8 fl.oz milk　**4 oz shredded suet**
5 oz self raising flour　**2 oz fresh white breadcrumbs**
1 rounded teaspoon baking powder　**1 egg, beaten**

Grease a 2 to 2½ pint pudding basin. Put the chopped figs and milk into a saucepan, bring to the boil and stew gently for about 5 minutes. Meanwhile, sift the flour and baking powder together into a bowl and mix in the sugar, suet and breadcrumbs. Make a well, pour in the milk/fig mixture and beat well together to combine thoroughly. Mix in the beaten egg and put the mixture into the pudding basin. Cover with greaseproof paper and cover and seal with kitchen foil. Steam for about 2 to 2½ hours, topping up the water as necessary. Turn out and serve with custard. Serves 4 to 6.

Baked Jam Roll

This baked suet pudding has a nice crisp, brown exterior with a soft jam-filled centre.
Mincemeat, marmalade or lemon curd are alternative fillings.

6 oz self raising flour
3 oz shredded suet
Water to mix
Jam, as preferred

Set oven to 400°F or Mark 6. Grease a large ovenproof dish. First make the suet pastry. Mix the flour and suet together in a bowl and then mix in just sufficient cold water to make a firm, not sticky, dough. Roll out the pastry to about ¼ inch thick on a lightly floured surface to form a strip 8 to 10 inches long. Spread a good layer of jam (warmed if necessary) over the pastry to within ½ to 1 inch of the edges. Moisten the edges of the pastry, roll up carefully from a long side and seal the edges well. Place in the dish and bake for about 30 minutes until nicely browned. Serve hot or cold, cut in slices, with custard. Serves 4 to 6.

Alternatively, the mixture can be rolled up in a floured pudding cloth and steamed for about 2½ to 3 hours to make Jam Roly Poly.

Folkestone Pudding Pie

Neither a pudding nor a pie but a tart baked with a
lemon-flavoured Bakewell-type filling topped with currants.

8 oz shortcrust pastry	**1 oz butter**
¾ oz ground rice	**1 tablespoon sugar**
½ pint milk	**1 egg, beaten**
Grated rind of 1 lemon	**2 oz currants**
Grated nutmeg for topping	

Set oven to 400° F or Mark 6. Grease a 7 inch flan dish. Roll out the pastry on a floured surface and line the dish, trimming the edge. Mix the ground rice with a little of the cold milk. Heat the rest of the milk with the lemon rind, in a pan over a low heat. Add the butter and ground rice mixture to the hot milk and stir until it thickens. Add the sugar and stir until it has dissolved. Allow to cool slightly then whisk in the beaten egg. Pour the mixture into the pastry case and scatter the currants over the surface. Bake for 10 minutes then reduce oven to 300ºF or Mark 2 and continue baking for about a further 20 minutes until golden and set. Serve with custard. Serves 4 to 6.

"Stir-in" Pudding

Any fruit can be used in this steamed sponge pudding, but
rhubarb or gooseberries are the most traditional.

12 oz self raising flour   Pinch of salt   6 oz butter, softened
½ lb prepared fruit: gooseberries, topped & tailed or rhubarb, trimmed and chopped
4 oz sugar (or to taste, according to the fruit)
1 egg, beaten   Milk to mix

Well butter a 2 to 2½ pint pudding basin. Sift the flour and salt together into a bowl then rub in the butter. Mix in the prepared fruit with the sugar (according to taste) then stir in the beaten egg with sufficient milk to form a fairly thick mixture. Spoon into the basin, cover with buttered greaseproof paper and cover and seal with kitchen foil. Steam for 2½ to 3 hours, topping up the water as necessary. Turn out on to a warm plate and serve with cream or custard. Serves 4 to 6.

Blackcap Pudding

Originally made with an old fashioned, almost black variety of raspberry rarely found these days, this light sponge pudding is now more usually topped with a cap of slightly stewed blackcurrants.

**½ lb blackcurrants, topped and tailed   2 teaspoons lemon juice   1 oz sugar
4 oz flour   ½ teaspoon baking powder
4 oz fresh white breadcrumbs   1 teaspoon grated lemon rind
2 eggs, beaten   ½ pint milk**

Well butter a 2 pint pudding basin. Rinse and lightly drain the blackcurrants and place in a dampened saucepan with the lemon juice and sugar. Cook very gently for 5 to 10 minutes, then spoon into the pudding basin. Sift the flour and baking powder together in a bowl, then mix in the breadcrumbs, sugar and lemon rind. Stir in the eggs, then add the milk and stir until combined well. Leave to stand in a cool place for 15 minutes, then pour over the blackcurrants. Cover with buttered greaseproof paper and cover and seal with kitchen foil. Steam for 2 to 2½ hours, topping up the water as necessary. Turn out and serve with custard or whipped cream. Serves 4 to 6.

Huntingdon Pudding

This steamed suet pudding is filled with gooseberries.
It is also known in Hertfordshire and Essex.

6 oz self raising flour	**4 fl.oz milk**
3 oz shredded suet	**8 oz green gooseberries, topped & tailed**
2 oz caster sugar	**2 oz brown sugar (or more to taste)**

Grease a 2 to 2½ pint pudding basin. In a bowl, mix together the flour, suet and caster sugar with sufficient milk to produce a dropping consistency. Put a layer of pudding mixture in the basin, cover with gooseberries and sprinkle with sufficient brown sugar. Repeat and finish with a layer of pudding mixture. Cover with buttered greaseproof paper and cover and seal with kitchen foil. Steam for 2½ to 3 hours, topping up the water as necessary. Serve from the basin with cream or custard. Serves 4.

Monmouth Pudding

In Victorian times, bread based puddings were considered ideal fare for children and for adults with delicate digestions. Monmouth Pudding reveals bold red and white stripes when served.

¾ pint milk   Grated rind of 1 lemon
1 oz butter   6 oz fresh white breadcrumbs
1 oz sugar   3 egg yolks
4-5 tablespoons strawberry jam

Set oven to 350°F or Mark 4. Grease a large ovenproof dish. Put the milk in a saucepan, add the butter, sugar and grated lemon rind and bring to the boil. Put the breadcrumbs in a bowl and pour the hot milk mixture over them. Allow to cool and swell. Stir the egg yolks into the cooled bread mixture and then spread half of the mixture over the base of the dish. Warm the jam, pour half of it over the mixture, add the remaining breadcrumb mixture and finish with a layer of jam. Bake for 40 to 45 minutes until set. Serves 4.

Ginger Marmalade Pudding

A variation of bread and butter pudding. If possible, use home-made marmalade.

5-6 slices wholemeal bread, crusts removed   Butter, as required
2 oz sultanas   2-3 oz Demerara sugar
Ginger marmalade   1 large egg, beaten   ½ pint milk
Demerara sugar and grated nutmeg, for sprinkling

Set oven to 350ºF or Mark 4. Grease a 1 to 1½ pint pie dish. Butter 2 or 3 slices of bread and use to line the bottom and sides of the dish. Sprinkle over a layer of sultanas and sugar. Spread a slice of bread thickly with marmalade and cover the fruit layer. Repeat with layers of fruit and bread and marmalade, finishing with a little sugar on top. Beat together the egg and milk and strain over the pudding. Leave for about 15 minutes to soak in. Sprinkle with brown sugar and grated nutmeg and bake for 40 to 50 minutes. Serve with cream. Serves 4.

Marquis Pudding

A layered pudding of apricot jam, stewed apples and creamy boiled rice with a ground almond topping.

1 lb cooking apples, peeled, cored and sliced
Sugar to taste   1 pint milk   1½ oz long grain rice
4 oz caster sugar   5 fl.oz double cream
4 oz apricot jam   3 oz ground almonds   1 egg

Set oven to 350ºF or Mark 4. Stew the apples with just a very little water and with sufficient sugar to taste, until soft. Meanwhile, bring the milk to boil in a pan, stir in the rice and simmer gently for about 40 minutes until cooked. Sweeten with 1 oz of the sugar and leave to cool slightly. Half whip the cream and combine with the rice. Put a layer of jam in the base of a deep pie dish, then a layer of stewed apples followed by a layer of rice. Repeat until the dish is about two thirds full. Mix the ground almonds with the remaining 3 oz sugar in a bowl, mix in the beaten egg and spoon small peaks of the mixture over the top layer of rice. Bake for about 35 minutes until lightly browned. Serve with warmed apricot jam flavoured with brandy. Serves 6.

Cherry Pudding

A plain sponge pudding filled with glacé cherries, which can be either steamed or baked.

4 oz butter, softened   **4 oz flour**
4 oz sugar   **Pinch of salt**
2 eggs, beaten   **3 oz glacé cherries**

Grease a 2 pint pudding basin. Cream the butter and sugar together in a bowl until light and fluffy. Beat in the eggs a little at a time with a little flour and then fold in the remaining flour and salt. Rinse the glacé cherries in cold water, dry well and cut in half. Combine the cherries with the sponge mixture and put into the basin. Cover with buttered greaseproof paper and cover and seal with kitchen foil. Steam for 1½ to 2 hours, topping up the water as necessary. Turn out on to a warm plate and serve with jam or custard. Serves 4 to 6.

Alternatively, set oven to 375°F or Mark 5. Put the mixture into a greased baking dish and bake for about 30 minutes until a skewer inserted comes out clean.

METRIC CONVERSIONS

The weights, measures and oven temperatures used in the preceding recipes can be easily converted to their metric equivalents. The conversions listed below are only approximate, having been rounded up or down as may be appropriate.

Weights

Avoirdupois	Metric
1 oz.	just under 30 grams
4 oz. (¼ lb.)	app. 115 grams
8 oz. (½ lb.)	app. 230 grams
1 lb.	454 grams

Liquid Measures

Imperial	Metric
1 tablespoon (liquid only)	20 millilitres
1 fl. oz.	app. 30 millilitres
1 gill (¼ pt.)	app. 145 millilitres
½ pt.	app. 285 millilitres
1 pt.	app. 570 millilitres
1 qt.	app. 1.140 litres

Oven Temperatures

	°Fahrenheit	Gas Mark	°Celsius
Slow	300	2	150
	325	3	170
Moderate	350	4	180
	375	5	190
	400	6	200
Hot	425	7	220
	450	8	230
	475	9	240

Flour as specified in these recipes refers to plain flour unless otherwise described.